LIKE IT OR NOT
Gavin Ewart

Illustrated by Ronald Ferns

RED FOX

A Red Fox Book

Published by Random House Children's Books
20 Vauxhall Bridge Road, London SW1V 2SA

A division of Random House UK Ltd.

London Melbourne Sydney Auckland
Johannesburg and agencies throughout
the world

First published by The Bodley Head Children's Books 1992

Red Fox edition 1993

Copyright © text Gavin Ewart 1992
Copyright © illustrations Ronald Ferns 1992

The rights of Gavin Ewart and Ronald Ferns to be
identified as the author and illustrator of this
work has been asserted by them in accordance
with the Copyright, Designs and Patents Act,
1988.

This book is sold subject to the condition that it
shall not, by way of trade or otherwise, be lent,
resold, hired out, or otherwise circulated without
the publisher's prior consent in any form of bind-
ing or cover other than that in which it is published and without a similar condition including
this condition being imposed on the subsequent
purchaser.

Printed and bound in Great Britain by
Cox & Wyman Ltd, Reading, Berkshire

ISBN 0 09 910521 7

Contents

Joe	7
Traffic Fumes	8
Crossing Main Roads	9
Summer Excursions	10
Winter Excursions	11
Late	12
Soup Song	13
Used to	14
Christmas	15
Unwanted	16
Ice-cream	17
Fireworks	19
Shopping Expeditions	19
Rain	20
Fry-up	22
Noise	23
Liking Red Hair	23
The Voice of Wisdom	24
The Black Death	25
School Plays	26
Miss Amberley	28
Ill	30
Model Craft	31
Bad Dreams	32
Pleasant Dreams	35
Snooker Ambitions	36
Laying New Carpets	37
The White Dwarf	39
Football	40
Wanting to be	41

Dos and Don'ts	41
Telly	42
Love/Hate	42
Bad Mood	43
Mr Macready	45
I Love Singing	46
Toffee	47
Snow	48
After the Snow	49
Cats	50
Cat Fluff	51
Who Likes the Idea of Guide Cats?	52
Footprints in the Snow	53
No Smoking	54
Annoying	55
Being Made to Show Off	56
Being Talked About	57
Flying Kites	59
Water Babies	60
What People Think About Children	61
Going Places	61
Doreen	62
As Long as it's Nice	64

Joe

I like Joe,
why I don't know,
but I like Joe!
He's as thin as a rake,
he's as thin as a hoe,
he doesn't run
like Sebastian Coe,
can't catch a cricket ball,
can't even throw!
He isn't bright –
but he's all right.
Make no mistake,
I like Joe!

Traffic Fumes

At the height we're at,
we're not too far from the lead in the petrol!
Which, all the scientists explain,
isn't very good for the brain.

Crossing Main Roads

Crossing main roads, however it's done,
never is very much fun.
The idiots dodge their way through the cars –
they're truly loonies, best behind bars!

Respect the Warden's helpful bossing.
Always use a Zebra Crossing!

Summer Excursions

Going out somewhere is always fun:
swimming, splashing, diving in the hot, hot sun!
But grandpas and grandmas like to keep cool.
They don't jump about in the swimming pool!

Winter Excursions

Museums are good, when there's snow and rain.
We can see the dinosaurs again!
See them move, and hear them roar!
Everyone adores a dinosaur.

Late

I don't like watches,
I don't like clocks,
I don't like struggling
to pull on my socks.

I'm the one they wait for,
they always have to wait,
because, for anything at all,
I'm always, always LATE!

I spend my life in rushing,
I never can catch up –
I'd win a Prize for Lateness,
I'd win a Challenge Cup.

I don't like whistles,
buzzers, bells or chimes.
I've been late for everything
about a thousand times!

Soup Song

There's thick soup, thin soup,
fresh soup, tin soup.
Mum makes it fresh; you'd be surprised
how many vegetables can be liquidized!

There's clear soup, dark soup;
very-wide-of-the-mark soup;
but Mum's is hot and thick and strong,
worth every kind of praiseful song!

There's fish soup, meat soup,
commercial heat-and-eat soup;
great admiration is evinced
at all the meats that Mum has minced!

There's leek soup, duck soup,
turkey-down-on-its-luck soup;
Mum's always gives you that cheerful glow –
you feel you'd walk ten miles through snow!

Used to

When we used to go
to Frittering-on-Sea
Grandpa always used to say
how it wasn't what it used to be!

There used to be a band
playing music in a bandstand,
and there used to be a race-course
with a covered-in Grand Stand.

But really I don't much care
what there used to be –
as long as there's sand and swimming
in a beautiful warm sea!

Christmas

Christmas is a holiday,
and not a melancholy day.

There's nothing more pleasant
than being given a present.

And Santa Claus's art is
the art of giving parties.

– But don't forget the poor ones
and the homeless out-of-door ones!

You might be happy, and having a ball,
but Christmas is meant for one and all.

Unwanted

There are some people
I wouldn't want to be –
like old Mr Crumhorn
or bad-tempered Mrs Peppercorn.
I'd never want *them* to be me!

Ice-cream

When the ice-cream man
with his ice-cream van
plays his simple tune,
we all gather round
at that joyful sound,
on a summer afternoon.

Make up your mind, quick!
There's money to find . . . Quick!
What is it going to be?
Desire for a cornet
stings me like a hornet –
how I wish all the ices were free!

Fireworks

When the fireworks are flashing and fizzy
their boisterous banging makes me quite dizzy.

Shopping Expeditions

When Mum takes us out to buy clothes
a big thrill, from my head to my toes,
goes through me!

Trying on is a special thrill.
It could never make me feel depressed or ill
or gloomy!

Rain

I hate rain!
The way it makes everything wet!
And comes back again and again,
so that we almost forget
what it is to have
a clear blue sky
and everything dry!

But no, we have to have
days and days of *rain*!
For hours and hours!

The only things that really enjoy rain
are the vegetables and the flowers –

but for me and for everyone else
rain is a pain!

Fry-up!

When Mum says
'We're going to have a Fry-Up!'
Golly! How
my spirits fly up,
no mistake,
I feel like a Wedding
in the Land of Cake!

When Mum says
'I feel like doing a Fry-Up!'
I feel great
as any High-Up,
no mistake,
I feel like an Ice-Cream
with a Chocolate Flake!

When Mum says
'It's time to have a Fry-Up!'
all my tears
quite quickly dry up,
no mistake,
nothing beats a Fry-Up –
no, nothing you could ever
broil or boil or bake!

Noise

I like noise,
we all like noise –
my elder sister
wants to be 'refined'
and to have 'poise'.
She and Mum often say:
'Why can't you be *quiet?*'

Dad says:
'You lot sound like a flipping riot!'

Liking Red Hair

I like all redheads,
copperknobs,
gingernuts,
red hair that's dark and marmalady,
or – with greater clarity –
light and carrotty!

But I'm particularly fond
of the girl they call
a strawberry blonde!

The Voice of Wisdom

Of course it's very sad
when your best friend says to you:
'Go away! You're completely mad!'

But don't lose hope!
In life, one finds,
best friends can change their minds!

The Black Death

I hate oil slicks
that cover the sea,
like a huge tongue that licks
all the living things away,
spreading like a tree . . .

birds with black wings
that struggle and sink,
fish, seals and all the things
that grow in bright colours, deep
black – as black as ink!

School Plays

Acting in plays
is one of the things
I really like best!
The robes and the rings
of the Three Christmas Kings
fill me with zeal and with zest!

And a Fairy Queen
or a Pirate King
or a Horrible Witch
have a wonderful zing –
it's an end-of-term thing
and we pray as we sing:
May it all go off
without a hitch!

Miss Amberley

On cold winter days
I don't like Miss Amberley!
It's because of her nose,
it's redder than a rose
or the Generals at Camberley –
and it's terribly long.
It goes on for ever
in the wintery weather!

Ill

I rather like being ill –
not *terribly* ill, but just a little bit ill,
lying in bed all warm and cosy,
after a tummy-ache or a chill!

The most pleasing thing about it
that I could mention
is that I'm the centre
of attention!

Model Craft

On lakes, ponds, meres and moats
serious men are sailing boats,
wearing waders. Remote control
helps them navigate with heart and soul.

Yachts do well if the winds don't fail –
adjust the rudder or shorten sail.
They make landfalls all admire.
Turn them round at your own desire.

Destroyers, speedboats, MTBs,
the pond's as vast as the Seven Seas,
passenger liners, clippers, dhows
sail in a landscape of creeks and cows.

All details correct, as in the books.
The men have poles, with controlling hooks.
They owe nothing to toyshop shelves –
they've made their models alone, themselves!

NOTE MTBS are Motor Torpedo Boats, as used by the Royal
Navy in World War II. The dhow is the traditional boat of
the Arabs.

Bad Dreams

The dreams that frighten so many, where
you're running and running and you don't get
   anywhere –
though you know
that a horrible Something is on your heels –
these are the dreams
that you wake from with screams
and terrible squeals!

Pleasant Dreams

The best dreams are about doing things
without even trying.
For instance, best of all,
the dreams of flying!
You can shoot about all over the place
or just hover –
without any bother!

Snooker Ambitions

Look, and you will see,
how the snooker referee
(or the marker, or whatever he's called)
has a head that's shiny and bald.

They never want to be
emperors or kings in marble halls –
what they would like to be most
is: billiard balls!

Laying New Carpets

When the Carpet Men come
it has a bad effect on Mum –
she gets very nervous
and there's a feeling of *Lord, preserve us!*

As they trample about with big feet
her anxiety is complete.
Will they knock the paint off the walls,
or kick the doors like footballs?

All her fears are very much alive –
will the furniture survive?
Like an invasion by the Goth or the Hun,
carpeting's not Mum's idea of fun!

The White Dwarf

Oh, beware of the White Dwarf!
His hair is completely white
and he only comes out at night,
he is full of wickedness and Oriental lore –
just thinking about him makes my mind sore!

And beware of his wife, the Black Dwarf!
Beware even more!
She is full of black hate to the core,
like a small hard black apple.
Any child that falls into her hands
or sits in *her* lap'll
end up as dead as a doornail in a door!

Football

I like playing football with the boys.
I like running, passing, shooting.
Dad says I'm a natural athlete.
Who cares about cheering, booing, hooting?

I just get on with the game.
Football's as rough as you like to make it.
I'm strong – and skilful –
and I can take it!

Wanting to be

I'd like to be a pop-star
or a television comic,
and I'd rather be
a cup of tea
than a bomb that is atomic!

Dos and Don'ts

I hate being told:
Do this! Do that!
or being pushed around
like a dog or a cat.

And to every bossy
bad-tempered *Don't!*
I answer *I will!*
and never *I won't!*

Telly

When Dad watches cricket or football
we creep around like zombies, every footfall
can hardly be heard, we're like little mice . . .
well, if you like football – like *him* – it's very
   nice!

Love/Hate

Sometimes I like Kate,
sometimes I hate her.
It's always one or the other.
I never have a balanced view of Kate.
Nor (I think) does her mother.

Bad Mood

When I get up in the morning
and I'm in a bad mood
I don't feel like eating or drinking
or eating my food.

So I take it out on the others –
that's the way it ends.
I spend the rest of the day just
annoying my friends.

Mr Macready*

Mr Macready
is horribly greedy –
he started off pretty big –
he eats and drinks hugely,
he's living in Rugeley.
He's as big
as a pig and a pig and a pig!

* Apologies to all men called Macready
who live in Rugeley, Staffordshire.

I Love Singing

When I'm singing
I feel like a Prince –
though those around me
cringe and wince!

Only the tone-deaf
are quite immune –
for I don't often
sing in tune.

Lots of wrong notes
throng the air.
But I love singing –
I don't care!

Toffee

Everybody loves toffee.
It's an addiction, like tea or coffee.
Once you've started you can never stop . . .

You're stuck in a sticky sea that's beachless.
You can't whistle or sing, and
it leaves you speechless!

Snow

I don't like snow in the streets,
it gets churned grey and black,
slipperier and mushier!

If you want clear, bright snow
the only place to go
is the very middle of Russia!

There it's clean, it's never dirty –
but the temperature is *minus* 30!

After the Snow

After the snow goes
you find the little snowdrops and crocuses
in clumps and in rows –

in winter's long storm,
under the ice and the hail and the blizzarding,
they have kept warm.

Optimists of *It might* and *It may*,
they knew the milder, more comfortable, weather
was coming their way!

Cats

I don't go for prize cats
or oversize cats –
or for stuck-up bad-tempered
stuffy cats,
huffy cats,
or very very fluffy cats!
The Champion Persian
is not my favourite version.

I like ordinary cats,
even slightly shabby cats –
black, black-and-white, tortoiseshell, ginger
and tabby cats!

Cat Fluff

Mum loves the cats
but she hates cat fluff –
it gets on the carpets and furniture,
it's terrible stuff.

It's because they moult
when the warm weather comes;
though sometimes it's because they fight.
Dad sits and hums.

He's neutral in the campaign
to keep the flat cat-fluff-free.
He says you can't have cats without cat fluff . . .
that seems good sense to me.

Who Likes the Idea of Guide Cats?

Of course, we have Guide Dogs For The Blind,
and we also have Girl Guides –
but why do Guide *Cats* never come to mind?
There would be protests on all sides

if we ever let *them* be our leaders!
Almost at once, we should be lost!
Even the cat-lovers, those special pleaders,
would admit the terrible cost

of letting cats, on our journeys, be in charge.
Animals that, with no warning, can go to sleep
on their way somewhere! Cats, small or large,
that all of a sudden run wild and leap,

chasing the leaves, or even chasing the flies –
it would be silly to give *them* any responsibility.
They can't be trained like dogs (that's no surprise).
Train a cat if you can! It's a rare ability!

Footprints in the Snow

When the cats make tracks,
there's just one set of tracks ...

When they jump from the window
they put their feet in the same places.

This proves, as you ought to know,
that cats don't like snow.

No Smoking

The incisors of the beaver
are very dark dark brown –
like the teeth of any smoker
in any major town!

But the beaver's not a puffer,
he does *not* pollute the skies.
He does *not* make others suffer.
The beaver's very wise.

Annoying

I like annoying people,
the good-as-gold and cloying people –
too good to be true!
I hate the goody-goodies,
Snow Whites, Little Red Riding Hoodies.
What about you?

Being Made to Show Off

My sister and I both play the piano.
We can play duets.
So whenever the uncles and aunts are around,
we're treated like performing pets!

We have to play our little pieces
like goody-goody child star nieces.

It's enough to make us, and *you*, sick!
It really puts the 'sick' in m*usic*!

Being Talked About

I hate it when old people say:
'He gets taller every day!'
I want to shout out, 'Ow!'
when they say, 'Such a big boy now!'
It really gets in my hair
when they talk about me as if I wasn't there.

Flying Kites

Flying kites is real fun
if your dad's good at it –
or your mum or another
big sister or brother.

Our dad wouldn't beat
Red Riding Hood at it!
Going up? Loop-the-looping?
No! It's down to the ground
all *his* kites are swooping!

Water Babies

I've got a friend called Norm.
He hates all swimming, he's afraid of water.
'A dying duck in a thunderstorm',
that's Norm at the Baths.
Any kind of murder, any kind of slaughter,
is what it sounds like, when *he* puts in a toe.
You'd think a shark had got him, if you didn't
   know.

What People Think About Children

Some people have called us sunbeams
and thought of us as perfect,
worth a fortune.
Others say we're worth only a few pence –
only a few cents.

But Dad just says we're a perfect nuisance!

Going Places

Going somewhere is fun.
Cars, trains, planes.
Getting there is just as exciting –
sometimes even more exciting –
than actually being there. In the long run.

Doreen

I don't like Doreen*!
She's got a pig face.
What's more, it's a big face.
There's far too much of it.
I don't like the look
or the shape
or the touch of it!

* Substitute, if you want to, the name of anyone you
  don't like.

As Long as it's Nice

I'll eat anything
as long as it's nice
I'll meet anyone
as long as they're very nice!
Anything, everything,
don't ask me twice –
I like anything
as long as it's nice!